Investor Relations – The Art of Communicating Value

Four Basic Steps to a Successful IR Program &
Creating the Ultimate Communications Platform

Jeffrey Corbin

If you are a C-Level executive or partner interested in submitting a manuscript to the Aspatore editorial board, please email jason@aspatore.com. Include your book idea, your biography, and any additional pertinent information.

Published by Aspatore, Inc.

For corrections, company/title updates, comments or any other inquiries, please email info@aspatore.com.

First Printing, 2004

10 9 8 7 6 5 4 3 2 1

ISBN 1-58762-981-X Library of Congress Control Number: 2004105584

Material in this book is for educational purposes only. This book is sold with the understanding that neither any of the authors or the publisher is engaged in rendering medical, legal, accounting, investment, or any other professional service. For legal advice, please consult your personal lawyer. This book is printed on acid free paper.

The views expressed by the individuals in this book do not necessarily reflect the views shared by the companies they are employed by (or the companies mentioned in this book).

About ASPATORE BOOKS –
Publishers of C-Level Business Intelligence

www.Aspatore.com

Aspatore Books is the largest and most exclusive publisher of C-Level executives (CEO, CFO, CTO, CMO, Partner) from the world's most respected companies. Aspatore annually publishes a select group of C-Level executives from the Global 1,000, top 250 professional services firms, law firms (Partners & Chairs), and other leading companies of all sizes. C-Level Business Intelligence™, as conceptualized and developed by Aspatore Books, provides professionals of all levels with proven business intelligence from industry insiders – direct and unfiltered insight from those who know it best – as opposed to third-party accounts offered by unknown authors and analysts. Aspatore Books is committed to publishing a highly innovative line of business books, and redefining such resources as indispensable tools for all professionals.

Investor Relations –
The Art of
Communicating Value

CONTENTS

A special thanks to all of those who consulted with me and assisted in the preparation of this book – to my partner Todd Fromer for his great IR expertise, to Bonnie Stretch for her mastery of the English language, to all of KCSA's publicly traded clients for providing us with the opportunity to share in their successes and work with them through difficult times and to my loving family for standing by my side and bearing with me during those late nights and vacations when this book required by attention.

- **Jeffrey Corbin**

Introduction

The Scene: A meeting of Jane, CFO of "Acme Corporation," and John, the company's Investor Relations Officer

CFO: John, over the past several months our stock has dropped nearly 20 percent. We need to get out there and tell our story to get our stock price up.

IRO: But Jane, even with a $20 stock price, Acme Corporation still trades at a 50x P/E ratio.

CFO: What's your point, John? Are you suggesting that we aren't undervalued and that our stock price can't go higher?

IRO: No – I'm just concerned that if we go out and speak with the Street, we might open ourselves up to short-sellers.

CFO: Then you better make sure that we don't introduce ourselves to the wrong investors. And you better make the case for why our stock should be worth more.

IRO: But Jane, our industry P/E is 30 and none of our competitors trade higher than that.

CFO: Well, isn't it your job to position ourselves and to communicate our growth story so that investors understand why our company presents the ultimate in investment opportunities and our P/E is appropriate. Are you up to the task?

The scene above may be fictional but the situation is not. Very often, the senior management team of any company – public or private – believes that their company's valuation should be higher than its current market capitalization or the price they are being offered for the purchase of their company. For many, the subject of valuation becomes so personal that all objectivity is lost, and company insiders, because they are so close to their work, completely lose perspective about the worth of their company and the reasons for its market valuation.

For the publicly traded company, it is important to recognize that the stock market works – that it presents a true valuation of a company. Multiply the company's stock price by the number of shares outstanding and there you have that company's valuation – its market capitalization. A publicly traded company's financial fundamentals speak for themselves. If a company is performing, shows strong revenue and earnings growth and management conveys a sense of trust, confidence and commitment to their business, investors will place an appropriate and accurate value on these factors as well as the risks associated with them. And this will be reflected in the company's stock price and overall valuation.

For the private company, given the fact that its equity is not liquid, valuation is not as simple and can be based on a multitude of factors including how similar public companies are valued, what the potential for cost savings in a post-merger setting might be and the strategic value of the company to a buyer. Nevertheless, the essence of a privately held company's valuation is the price an arms-length purchaser is willing to pay. The financials of the private entity, the extent to which a prospective purchaser believes there is a likelihood of continued success, and an understanding of the opportunity within the industry, are factors that will be considered when valuing the company and making an offer to purchase it.

While execution is key to a company's success, the way in which a company, public or private, *communicates* the essential factors to a potential investor or purchaser is central to the price which that individual will likely be willing to pay. If vital elements are omitted from a company's story, or if they are not told convincingly and with veracity, true value will most likely not be recognized.

Investor relations – the art of positioning and communicating a company's story and investment proposition to investors – is the heart and soul of attaining fair value. For the company that trades at a price-to-earnings multiple less than that of its peers, or that sits on cash which is greater than its market capitalization, the proper communication of that company's strengths and growth potential is key to demonstrating that the company is undervalued. For the company that trades at a premium to its current industry P/E multiple (e.g. Acme Corporation), the way in which that company communicates how it intends to grow faster than its competition and how the market opportunity will allow it to execute on its growth strategy is essential to maintaining its current valuation or increasing it

However, if a company's communications – in writing or in oral presentations – do not sufficiently explain the current valuation and potential opportunity, the highest possible valuation will not be attained and, as will be discussed further in Chapter I, more damage than good may in fact result.

There *is* a method to communicating value effectively. And, regardless of whether a company is public or private, it can be accomplished in four basic steps:

- Step 1: Determine the investment proposition a company presents.

- Step 2: Identify and target the appropriate investor audience.

- Step 3: Develop the communications platform to present to the targeted investor audience.

- Step 4: Build relationships with the targeted investor audience and maintain consistent communications with the marketplace so the key value drivers of a company's business are current and obvious to investors.

Having represented companies of all market capitalizations, from all industries and on all stock markets for more than 35 years, it can be said with confidence that these steps form the foundation for the practice of investor relations. For the companies that follow them, measurable results will be delivered in the form of heightened credibility, greater access to capital and most important – an accurate valuation.

1

Four Steps to
Communicating Value

Step 1: Determining the Investment Proposition

Market Value versus Intrinsic Value

Before even considering going on the road and presenting a company's story to investors, a company must understand what type of investment opportunity it presents. A basic understanding of "market value" and "intrinsic value" therefore is in order.

The Oxford Dictionary defines valuation as "an estimation of something's worth." For the publicly traded company, where, in most cases, there is an opportunity to buy or sell stock in an open and liquid market, valuation is that company's market capitalization. Market capitalization is defined by Barron's Dictionary of Finance and Investment Terms as the "value of a corporation as determined by the market price of its issued and outstanding common stock." Based on these definitions, for the publicly traded company, valuation is nothing more and nothing less than the current price a buyer is willing to pay and a seller is willing to accept for a liquid, minority interest in a company. It is a company's "market value" today.

A company's market value or stock price is based on a broad array of factors as well as a large number of people. Assuming corporate information is disclosed in a fair and timely manner, at any given moment, a company's stock price will be determined by thousands of different investors, each with different expectations of a company's future performance. Taking into consideration each investor's unique investment protocols, diverse personal or business goals and varying levels of market experience, additional complexity to the valuation discussion abounds.

Having counseled hundreds of public companies with regard to the role of valuation in investor relations, many different elements affecting a company's valuation or market value exist. Nevertheless, in counseling the members of senior management, it is always necessary to focus on those elements that a company's management team can influence. And these include profitability, growth, cash flow generation and risk.

This brings us to the discussion of intrinsic value. Before explaining the difference between market value and intrinsic value, the point needs to be made that, except in the case of the investor who is looking to invest only in order to receive income through a guaranteed dividend payment, most investors will only invest in a company if the market value of that company is expected to appreciate. As stated before, market value is what a company is priced at today. A company's intrinsic value, on the other hand, is much more complex. It is what a company's market value is expected to be some time in the future. It involves utilizing different methods to determine what this value should be.

Determining a company's intrinsic value

Some investors value businesses based on expectations of future profits, future growth, future cash flow and future risk. Others focus on a company's asset value or break-up value. Still, others focus on a combination of both present and future criteria to determine an appropriate price for a minority interest in a public company. While different investors will weigh each of these measures differently when analyzing a company, at the end of the day they all seek to reach the same conclusion. Is this company worth more than its market value today? Or, do I believe management will create additional value in the future so that my investment will appreciate as the market recognizes a greater worth?

Determining how investors reach their varying conclusions of intrinsic value is what drives the practice of investor relations. And, as shall be discussed later in this book, the way in which a company communicates its story, in writing or verbally, is the basis on which investors will conclude a company's intrinsic value. Before communicating, it is therefore necessary for a company to understand how investors calculate intrinsic value. This involves an analysis of a company's profitability, growth, cash flow and risk – the focal points of valuation and the areas where management, through its actions, has the ability to create value for its shareholders.

Self-analysis or introspection is a necessary component in the long-term quest for a company to achieve its highest possible future valuation. In order to engage in this process, it is necessary that management teams understand the various valuation techniques employed by investors and analysts so that they can best determine their story and communicate the investment proposition that is unique to their company and that will best resonate with investors.

While Wall Street still suffers from a short-term orientation and fixation with earnings per share and accounting profit, based on discussions with hundreds of institutional investors and analysts, the most effective approach to determining a company's value is to conduct an analysis of cash flow. If a company has in place a new strategy to grow its business, cash flow will be the final arbiter of such a strategy's success. Important questions such as "to what extent is management using more cash than it is generating?" and "what reward will be recognized by a company's cash investments?" are now being asked more often by investors. And, the reason for this is simple – cash flow is a measure of operational and managerial effectiveness in all aspects of a business.

Value creation and the ability of a company to reach an appropriate and fair market valuation therefore requires sound decisions by management with regard to cash flow from operations as well as investing and financing activities. Companies that do not generate cash or cannot estimate when they will be able to do so will have the greatest difficulty explaining their intrinsic value (not to mention attracting investors). Cash flow is increasingly becoming a priority in investors' valuation models. Therefore, even if a company has great products and offers excellent services, unless it demonstrates that it is able to generate cash, today or in the near future, that company will have greater difficulty attracting investor dollars.

In addition to analyzing cash flow, there are other ways in which investors determine whether there is a discrepancy between a company's current market valuation and ultimate intrinsic value and whether greater future value exists in a company. While investors utilize varying benchmarks when analyzing and gauging their expectations of a company's performance or in determining its intrinsic value at any given point in time, and while these benchmarks may vary from industry to industry, the basic formulas that investors use to determine value are always tied to profitability, growth, cash flow and risk.

A company's investment proposition may also be tied to its value in relation to other investment opportunities. In most cases, a company's performance is gauged by its value relative to industry peers or competitors. However, when no clear comparable entity exists, a completely different class of investment may become the benchmark that investors use when valuing a company's investment proposition. In other words, if a company truly is unique and has no competitors, investors will look to other forms of investments (e.g. bond or index funds) as a basis to compare a company's growth rate and risk.

Growth and value as general investment propositions

Once a company has undergone the process of self-introspection to understand its intrinsic value and how it should ultimately be valued, it must then decide what type of investment opportunity it presents. It is this proposition that a company will eventually communicate to investors.

The type of investment opportunity a company presents usually boils down to two basic propositions – one of value and one of growth. Value investors rummage through the markets for stocks whose fundamentals and long-term prospects appear excellent but that are undervalued in relation to the company's intrinsic value. For example, a public company with liquid assets like cash and marketable securities in excess of its current market capitalization would be considered a value investment. Another example of a value opportunity would be a company (unlike Acme Corporation) that trades at a price/earnings multiple of ten times next year's expected earnings while the rest of the industry trades at an average of twenty times next year's earnings. Assuming its fundamentals and risk factors are reasonably similar to other companies in the industry, this company would be an appealing value opportunity.

There are many ways to analyze a company that represents a value proposition and every value investor has a different approach. Nevertheless, most value investors are interested in similar performance and valuation measures. Some of these include:

- Price/Book Value
- Price/Earnings Ratio
- Price/Cash Flow
- Enterprise Value/Free Cash Flow
- Enterprise Value/EBITDA
- Price/Cash
- DCF analysis (Discounted Cash Flow)

Simply put, value investors look for companies that have fallen out of favor or are under Wall Street's radar screen. A value manager's quest is to identify discrepancies between a company's current market capitalization and its intrinsic value. So, where a company has a market capitalization that is less than its current intrinsic value, this becomes the prime opportunity for the value investor.

The other investment proposition a company can present is one of growth. Growth companies are those that investors believe will grow their sales and earnings at a rate faster than the market or industry average. These are the companies that demonstrate that there is additional value waiting to be unleashed, that they have the ability to cause this to happen and that their company's intrinsic value should be greater than its current valuation.

Unlike value investors, growth investors identify their investment opportunities by looking at measures that include:

- PEG Ratio (PE/Growth Rate)
- P/E Expansion
- Earnings Growth
- Revenue Growth
- Relative Strength

While companies can be categorized as having either growth or value stories, the two are not mutually exclusive. In fact, for the company that appears overvalued based on a price/earnings multiple analysis, the ability of the company to grow need be considered when assigning an appropriate multiple. In the case of the fictional Acme Corporation, one might claim that, given an average P/E multiple of 30 for the industry, Acme Corporation is overvalued, as it trades at a P/E multiple of 50. Nevertheless, if Acme is likely to grow at a rate of more than 50% per annum and is able to communicate and convince an investor of this, then a multiple of 50 may be appropriate. And if this is so, Acme Corporation may even be able to make the case that it is undervalued. Indeed, if there should exist significant cash and little debt on Acme's balance sheet, Acme can make the case that its P/E ratio is lower than its peers when adjusted for cash. Therefore, Acme Corporation can offer investors both a growth and a value opportunity.

The point to be made is that in order to succeed in its investor relations activities, a company must first know who it is and what investment proposition it represents. It must first put itself through the process of self-introspection. Once this is done, it can then proceed to Step 2 and determine the proper investor audience.

Step II: Targeting the Right Investors

Many companies with great investment propositions are not properly valued by the marketplace. Many companies are definitely worthy of a higher valuation, but, for some reason, are not able to achieve it. Often the reason for this is quite simple. Management has not been proactive in its investor outreach and, as a result, no one knows the company exists.

In the United States there are thousands upon thousands of investors – mutual fund managers, hedge fund managers, asset managers and retail brokers – each with separate and unique investment philosophies. And, with thousands of companies to invest in, why should an investor pick one over the other? The answer to this is also quite simple. The company that has a communications platform that clearly conveys its investment proposition and a management team that gets out there to tell its story has the better chance of winning the investor race than the company that hibernates at its headquarters.

Take, for example, the case of the company that was trading at a stock price of nearly $1 per share. In fear of being delisted from the Nasdaq National Market, the company approached its investor relations consultant to learn what could be done to solve this looming problem. The answer was obvious. While the company was successfully executing on its business plan, no one knew it. The company had gone into seclusion and, for more than a year, had refrained from meeting investors. By getting out there, approaching investors and making them aware of the opportunity, investors were able to understand the intrinsic value waiting to be recognized. Within a year, such value was obtained.

Once a company completes Step I above and determines the investment proposition it represents, the next step is to determine the specific type of investor that should be made aware of it. On one level, investors *are* alike. Their central concerns focus on how much reward they will reap from their investment risk and how quickly this will happen. While investors are interested in what a company does for a living and the industry in which it exists, this information is only valuable if it helps to illuminate the likely return on their investment. The primary concern to investors is that the company in which they are investing is addressing a market opportunity that will increase the value of the money they are risking.

In choosing to buy stocks, all investors focus on the balance between risk and reward. But not all investors look at risk and reward the same way. To persuasively communicate future intrinsic value to a group of investors, it is essential to understand individual styles of investing. The following general categories describe some of the most common investment approaches:

- **Growth Investors.** Some individuals or firms invest only in companies that they believe have potential for rapid growth. In selecting companies, they focus on the income statement and are usually looking for annual growth that outpaces the overall market as well as investments with similar risk profiles.

- **Value Investors.** These investors look for companies whose share price is less than the company's asset value or that trade at multiples well below the industry average. They focus on the total balance sheet and believe that if a company is financially sound, they will be rewarded over time for buying in at an undervalued or "cheap" level. These investors also care about growth – they want to know what is likely to get the market's attention and how this will push up market value. But, paying a discounted market price for the company's intrinsic value is their main concern.

- **Momentum Investors.** These investors move in and out of stocks quicker than most. They are focused on catalysts in a business that will drive improved results and strong market reaction. These investors are likely to "ride the wave" of a strong product, a new discovery or an increasing industry trend. They will use a combination of value and growth to determine their entry and exit points but seldom stick around for the long term.

- **GARP Investors.** Some investors look for both value and growth. These investors are known as GARP investors and look for companies with Growth At a Reasonable Price. They look for bargains as value investors do. But they are less likely to invest solely on future growth. Rather they seek companies that trade at discounted multiples so they can capture the value and the longer-term growth opportunity. GARP investors will often sell when they feel a company has achieved a fair market value or multiple in line with its peers.

- **Markets and Industry Specialists.** Other investors specialize in particular industries or markets, for example, technology or health care. Still others limit their investments according to geography – they prefer companies located in certain regions of the United States. Others prefer companies that have an international component (e.g. emerging markets). These investors can be growth, GARP, value, momentum, income, etc.

- **Theme Investors.** These are investors that seek companies that will benefit from trends in an industry or the economy. Examples of such theme investors are those that invest in the banking sector where an increase in interest rates drives greater profitability or those that invest in precious metals companies as a result of strong pricing trends in the gold industry.

- **Income Investors.** Income investors are interested in a dividend. They want to know the size of the dividend, how long it has remained at the current amount, how often it is raised, and how long the company can afford to pay it.

Step II to successful investor relations requires that a company identify every group of potential investors that would be interested in its investment proposition. Take for example the Israeli technology company that sits on more cash than its current market capitalization of $50 million and plans to grow at a rate of 25 percent per year. This company's target investor pool should consist of numerous types of investors. It should consist of investors that invest in companies located in Israel; investors that invest in emerging markets; investors that invest in technology companies; investors that invest in micro-cap value companies; as well as investors that invest in micro-cap growth companies.

To exclude any of these groups of investors would be to preclude them from ever knowing the investment opportunity exists. On the other hand, to take this company to investors whose portfolio consists of large-cap industrial companies or those that invest only in U.S. companies would be an obvious mistake, not to mention a waste of time.

The type of investor that a company chooses to address or "target" is essential to its overall IR success and to achieving its highest possible valuation. Before meeting with any investor, it is essential that a company know the dynamic of that investor and fit within the profile of the type of company in which the investor invests. For the company that is clearly able to demonstrate and communicate a story of potential growth, the "growth" investor should be approached. However, for a growth company, such as Acme Corporation, to approach a "value" investor without a very convincing growth story in its arsenal could be a mistake, as many value investors may see Acme as overvalued and an ideal opportunity for shortselling.

With Steps One and Two complete, a company now knows who it is and who it should meet with.   It is now ready to consider conducting proactive investor outreach.   However, before doing so, it need have appropriate ammunition in place to communicate and explain to each investor why he or she should invest.   What a company says in its investor materials and verbal presentations will affect this determination. Step Three to successful investor relations requires that a company have materials that meet the needs of each investor, even if this means having multiple sets of materials and presentations.

Step III: Establishing the ultimate communications platform

For the company that only presents a growth investment proposition, that company's communications platform must exude "growth." For the value proposition company, the communications platform must trumpet the "undervalued" song. For the company that is growing by leaps and bounds and at the same time is undervalued, that company must tell its story in two ways.   When meeting with growth investors, it must demonstrate to the investor how it plans to grow. When meeting with value investors, it must explain the rationale for why it believes it is undervalued.   While it is not necessary to have two separate sets of materials or presentations, it is important that when this company meets with each of these two types of investors it know which one it is meeting with and tailor its remarks to each of their respective needs for information.

As mentioned above, for a company trading at a P/E multiple higher than its industry average to approach a value investor could subject that company to shortselling. These shortselling investors look for companies that are overvalued and, based on their analysis, should come down from their current market value. For the company that falls into this category, it would be a big mistake to approach value investors since they will immediately recognize the opportunity that exists to short the company's stock – unless, of course, that company can convincingly communicate how it is that it intends to grow at a rate faster than its industry competitors and why it deserves a P/E multiple higher than its industry. In the case of Acme Corporation, approaching value investors with a 50x P/E multiple when the industry average for its peers is 30 could be extremely damaging unless the company can clearly communicate how it intends to grow at a rate significantly higher than that of its competition. Unless management can persuade Wall Street that a clear opportunity for growth exists for the company and that its plan for execution is viable, investors are likely to question the company's high valuation and begin to short Acme's stock. And why shouldn't they? Savvy investors know that every company they meet has high expectations, but only a few can actually execute well enough to achieve their goals.

Acme Corporation must therefore set forth in its investor materials and presentation (also known as its communications platform) a clearly articulated foundation for growth with benchmarks explaining how that growth will be achieved. Investors want to understand the big picture and to feel confident that a company is focused and has a plan that it is following. Investors also want to be able to follow along with a company's growth. In this day and age of companies defrauding the public, it is not sufficient for a company simply to state in conclusory fashion that it plans to grow. Without clear explanation and discussion, investors will just not believe it.

A company's communications platform consists of every piece of written material it distributes to investors as well as every oral communication it makes. Having a communications platform that provides a roadmap for success is therefore necessary to demonstrate how a company believes that it can successfully execute and grow its company. A well thought out and comprehensive communications platform allows investors to realize that management is aware of its responsibility to provide as much information as possible to its current and prospective equity holders and to give them the confidence they need to feel comfortable parting with their cash and investing.

Chapter II of this book demonstrates in detail how a company can best present itself to fully recognize its intrinsic value as well as achieve its highest possible valuation. A company has various means in which to communicate how it intends to grow and why its current stock price or valuation is appropriate or why it should have a higher value. Management can provide investors with a snapshot of their business in the form of a **fact sheet** that highlights how they have positioned the company to grow and the opportunity for growth that exists in the industry. They also have the ability to speak to investors at investor conferences or meet with them in one-on-one or group settings. At these meetings, management can present a **PowerPoint investor presentation** that similarly highlights its growth potential.

Each year, Acme Corporation issues an **annual report**. Through this major communication vehicle, which has a one-year shelf life, the company's CEO can articulate how well management executed on its plan for the previous year and can discuss the company's plan for the coming year, providing benchmarks or "watchpoints" for investors to look for in the months to come. As the Company achieves each benchmark, it should highlight these in its **news announcements** and **quarterly earnings press releases** (as well as during **conference calls with investors**). Such communications not only demonstrate that the company is executing on its growth plan, but establish confidence among investors that Acme Corporation can achieve its goals, regardless of how ambitious they may be.

By using each of these communications formats to tell a consistent story and by professionally packaging them together as an **investor relations kit** as well as highlighting each of them in the **investor relations section of the company's website**, Acme Corporation can establish a communications platform that demonstrates the company's capability to grow faster than other companies in its industry, helping to justify its current P/E multiple.

Step IV: Building relationships with investors

With a sound investment proposition determined, an appropriate audience of investors targeted and a well articulated story found in a company's investment materials, the next step toward achieving success in a company's investor relations program is to secure a meeting with the right investor, convince the investor why he or she should invest and begin the process of building a relationship that will hopefully lead to the investor maintaining a long-term investment in the company.

The reality is that a company's fundamentals speak for themselves. Any investor can go to a Bloomberg terminal or speak to their analyst friend at Merrill Lynch or Lehman Brothers to learn the fundamentals of a company. By the time it begins its outreach activities, the company already has done the hard work of professionally summarizing the salient reasons why its stock makes for a prudent investment. All that now needs to be done is for the company to convince the potential investor that his investment will be in good hands.

And, this is the challenging part – convincing the investor that management is serious about its company, is in it for the long haul and has no intention of squandering the investor's cash. While many CEOs and CFOs have the requisite presentation skills, many are new to representing publicly traded companies and could benefit from pre-meeting rehearsal and training. The one thing an investor cannot get from Bloomberg, Merrill Lynch or Lehman Brothers is the personal flavor and emotions of management. So the way in which management presents itself at the meeting is crucial since management has only one opportunity to make its case.

The expression "rubbing the table" connotes trust and confidence building. It is the concept of sitting across the table from an investor, looking him or her in the eye and speaking with a style that conveys truth in performance and trust in management. It is about building relationships in addition to providing an opportunity for management to establish milestones for investors to keep an eye out for. It is one thing to lay out benchmarks to track a company's execution and growth. It is another thing to actually accomplish these goals. Investors require a basis on which to determine whether or not a company is delivering on its plan. Rubbing the table is an opportunity to accomplish just this. Trust is instilled by delivering on promises, thereby adding credibility to everything a company says and does.

* * *

The objective of any investor relations program is to build a base of long-term investors that believe in a company and its management team. While some might hope that as part of this process their stock will appreciate, the truth is that the real aspiration should be that their stock will attain its true and fair intrinsic value.

A carefully considered investor communications platform is at the heart of a company's effort to attain true value. What a company says about itself and how it says it is central to how that company will be perceived. The ability of a company to communicate persuasively depends on the company's ability to truly understand its strengths, where it is going, what type of investment opportunity it represents and, therefore, what type of investor to approach. While a company's financial fundamentals speak for themselves, what a company says and how it says it ultimately will determine how the market values its business.

Investor relations is not about the number of investors a company meets with or how aggressively a company promotes itself. It is about making the strongest case for its current market value and future intrinsic value. It is about effectively communicating this to the right investor audiences. Chapter II will now address the mechanics necessary to create the ultimate communications platform and establish the highest possible valuation.

2

Essential Tools for Communicating Value

New government regulations for accounting and corporate governance demand that information be communicated faster, more accurately, and more transparently – three goals that often seem mutually exclusive to harried business executives. But regardless of whether a company's story is one of growth or one of being undervalued in the market, there are certain communications tools that will help executives tell their company's story clearly, effectively, and in a timely manner.

Concise and consistent information is essential for building trust in today's business world. We live in an environment of rapid change and information saturation, and most people, investors included, have a short attention span. Too many companies are competing to be noticed. Therefore, each business achievement, each quarter's results, each strategic development should be communicated quickly, adding new information consistent and in context with the overall business strategy that investors and analysts have come to understand.

Every company has a story to tell. The more concise, consistent, clear and energetic management makes that story, the more likely investors will listen and understand.

Investors – and indeed, all key constituencies (analysts, the press, customers, employees, strategic partners among them) – need a clear understanding of a company's fundamental business focus. As equity owners, they not only have a need to know how management intends to grow the business, but also a right. Considering the fact that they are parting with their cash, they have the right to inquire, "How well are you going to be using this investment that you want from me? If I give you my money, will I get a good return on my investment?" These are fair questions, no doubt. And the best response is through frequent and accurate communications that demonstrate that the company is on track, meeting previously identified objectives, planning developments for the near future, and analyzing and explaining financial results.

Golden Rules of Good Communications

There are three golden rules of good communications that can be of vital help in building a foundation of trust and reputation for a company.

- *Be consistent* in describing the company, its goals and objectives, its achievements and its financials. No matter what the means of communications, say the same thing and remember that if you don't, someone, at some point in time, will call you on it.

- *Communicate often and in a timely fashion*, so that investors and potential stakeholders, financial analysts, reporters and other interested parties can see how the company is executing on challenges and opportunities. Whether the news is good or bad, management should be the first to communicate it. And even if it appears that there is no news to discuss, something of interest must be taking place to report and to demonstrate that the company is executing on a plan. Remember investors often consider silence to mean that management is asleep at the wheel.

• *Put each development in the context of the overall business strategy,* so the audience can see how individual events advance the overall plan. Do not shrink from discussing challenges that may arise; treat them as an opportunity to show how they will be met and overcome. Communicating the difficulties with the successes helps to build new confidence in executive integrity and managerial skill.

Tools You Can Use

Numerous tools exist for a company to communicate its value. As such, this chapter is divided into two sections:

Section A presents four major tools essential to communicating a company's business and development:

• **The Annual Report,** especially the **Shareholders' Letter** from the Chief Executive Officer.

• The SEC forms, especially **Forms 10K, 10Q** and **8K**

• **Press releases** about quarterly earnings and new business developments

• The **Conference Call**

Each of these standard tools presents communications opportunities that are often overlooked, even by experienced executives.

Section B focuses on *specialized, highly focused* and *easy-to-read documents* that quickly and succinctly differentiate the company from its competitors and position it strongly within its industry sector. These help not only to dynamically convey a company's potential and capture the attention of busy potential investors, but also to set the stage for why a company deserves a higher valuation. Such documents include:

● **A Fact Sheet** – a two-page investor-focused document that provides a brief yet detailed overview of the company.

● **A Corporate PowerPoint Investor Presentation**, including charts and graphs that visually communicate the company's financial development and growth potential, as well as a strong company overview consistent with that of the Fact Sheet.

● **An Investor Relations Kit**, which brings everything together – the entire communications platform – in one neat package.

Irrespective of the formality of these documents and means of communicating, one common theme underlies all. Every company has (or should have) a business plan. And, every company has (or should have) a growth strategy. To properly tell a company's story and to attract an investor audience, a company need convey its business plan and growth strategy in simple terms and in every mode of communication. This is not to suggest that a company reveal each and every of its innermost secrets. Rather, to lay out a foundation for what a company hopes to achieve in both the near and long term will provide investors with the comfort of knowing that the company is focused, has a goal in mind and also has a methodology for achieving success. As the company executes on this plan and announces developments in its business, investors will have the necessary roadmap in which to evaluate the company's success and to gauge whether their investment was and remains prudent.

SECTION A: THE ESSENTIAL COMMUNICATIONS TOOLS

Adding Value through the Annual Report and Shareholder Letter

The annual report is an important vehicle in which a company can communicate its business plan and make a case for its valuation. Annual reports can range from a simple "wrap-around" of the company's 10K for the year to an elaborate visual presentation of the company's products, services, technology, facilities, customers, partners and management team. Choices depend on what is cost effective for the individual company in question. Notice the key words are "cost *effective*," not "least expensive." The important question is what needs to be communicated most forcefully?

A Road Map for the Year

The annual report – and especially the indispensable element of the CEO or President's letter to shareholders – lays out for all constituencies the company's achievements and challenges of the past year and the road map of the business and operational goals for the year ahead. It is in this document that investors look for a clear, complete telling of the company's story.

Simple or complex, this is a major document that, if done correctly, can vividly communicate the fundamental strengths and long-term outlook of a business. It clarifies and makes more readable the message told in the official SEC documents. It simplifies the essence of the story and allows for personal commentary of the company's mission and vision. While the annual report should convey excitement about the company's achievements, the story should accurately take into account the factual financial information and risk factors enumerated in the 10K. Inconsistencies between what the story says and what the financial numbers reveal will raise a red flag for investors and government regulators alike. Moreover, the company that shows incredible enthusiasm in the President/CEO letter but delivers heaping losses without proper explanation will be looked upon with incredulity.

Nonetheless, the annual report is a company's most powerful communication document. It communicates visually as well as through words the character of a business. For example, if a business is young, and cost control is a central issue, the appearance of the annual report will convey that. Cost constraints may permit only a few photographs, and the text may rest primarily on the President/CEO Letter. On the other hand, if the company has made great gains in the previous year and it is important to communicate its growing leadership position within its industry, the graphic design of the annual report should convey that competitive power. Separate sections, with full-color photography and detailed texts, can be devoted to dramatically illustrating the importance of new products, customers, divisions or acquisitions, for example.

Regardless of the size of the company or its budget, creative use of graphics is an important tool in communicating the most essential points about a company's growth. The annual report need be looked at as a company's most important piece of marketing collateral. Even if large photographic spreads are out of keeping with the modest size and accomplishments of the company, clear financial graphs showing growth in revenue, net income, or shareholder's equity are simple but concise means to convey accurate information visually and memorably. If a new facility was opened during the past year, one or two good photographs will help to make that achievement more concrete and real for the reader. The cost of these graphics and visuals is minimal compared to their communication value and impact. This is what is meant by "cost effective."

Shareholder Letter: A Personal Communication.

The shareholder letter is one of the CEO's most important opportunities to speak directly to the company's shareholders – and by extension, to potential investors as well. The tone should be personal, conveying that the Chief Executive or President understands what the shareholder wants to know as well as that he or she is willing and able to answer the shareholders' most urgent concerns. Moreover, as the following excerpt from a shareholders letter demonstrates, this is an ideal forum in which to lay out not only all of the accomplishments of the previous year, but also a road map for the coming year and what investors can expect to see coming from the company.

> *While I'm thrilled to be reporting to you how well we've done, I'll let the numbers tell the rest of the story. For the moment, I'd like to take a few minutes to tell you about where I want this company to be this time next year.*
>
> *First and foremost, restaurants will continue to be our core offering throughout the upcoming year and years. We will continue to work diligently to ensure that our partners flourish through their association with us. We will build on our success in obtaining*

additional partners. Through our diligence, we forecast continued strong growth in this area.

While we will continue to grow our restaurant proposition, we also will be using our core competencies and broad marketing reach to expand into other vertical markets. We will launch a new hotel program with an initial roster of more than 300 high quality boutique hotels in top metro markets. By year-end we expect to offer rewards at thousands of hotels in 40 major business and leisure destinations.

The next vertical we will enter is the retail sector. We will spend this year researching the marketplace, understanding our member wants and needs and developing the plan for building a retail offering.

Concurrent with our aggressive goals in entering new vertical markets, we are also intent on expanding into other geographic markets. The coming year should see the launch of our presence in Canada, as we continue exploring our options north of the border.

As can be seen in this example, the CEO in this letter sheds light on the company's business plans, and, in particular, its growth strategy. She gives specific examples of what the company is working on and what investors should look out for in the company's news announcements.

Some management teams may look at such openness with skepticism, as they may believe that candor sets the stage for disappointment. And, this is a justified concern. Management does not want to say it is going to do something and then not deliver. However, in providing an outline for the future, such apprehension can be relieved if management keeps in mind the adage, "under-promise and over-perform." Truth be told, the company that provides the best path for future growth and substantiates this with successful execution will fare better than the company that discloses less. Shareholders are equity owners in a public company and have the right to have a basic understanding of what is taking place at their company.

Best practices for the ideal shareholders letter include the following elements:

• Open with "Dear Shareholders:" – This addresses the audience directly.

• Include a summary of financial results, including such comparables as quarter-over-quarter, year-over-year. Remember that the Sarbanes-Oxley Act requires that GAAP numbers precede pro forma numbers (see Chapter III).

• Discuss achievements and challenges of the past year.

• Discuss in some detail the long-term strategic growth plan and the portion of it that will be accomplished in the coming 12 months.

• Discuss goals and strategies to meet upcoming challenges to increase investor confidence.

• Present "watch points" by which investors can measure management's execution on its plan.

- Discuss methods of internal corporate governance and financial oversight to engender trust and promote truthfulness.

Telling the good and the bad.

It is important to be positive. There is nothing wrong with leading off with the year's best achievements – financial goals met; new products launched; and awards won for industry, business, or management achievement. But it is also necessary to acknowledge any shortfalls, to discuss what happened to cause these issues and how management expects to improve the situation in the coming year.

Take for example the company that was profitable for the year, made several accretive acquisitions, paid an increased dividend, but saw its revenues reduced by five percent when compared to the previous year. After discussing the financial results, the company in its President/CEO is wise to state:

> *The stalled economy in 2003 triggered lower demand for capital goods and generated excess capacity for companies selling into these markets. The decline in this sector resulted in reduced demand for the Company's products in certain markets, which contributed to the Company's record performance in the previous year.*
>
> *In addition to the general state of the economy, increases in the cost of employee health care, prescription drugs and insurance affected the Company's operating performance. Positive results stemmed from tightened operating budgets and cost-*

reduction programs at all subsidiaries and divisions. However, for the first time in fifteen years the Company did not experience increased sales and earnings.

Nevertheless, the Company increased the cash dividend, sustaining a record of dividend increases for 20 consecutive years.

The current level of uncertainty in an already stagnant economy suggests that the upcoming year could be another soft year, particularly for companies in our industry.

By being forthright, this not only will address SEC concerns but also will raise investors' confidence in management's sense of corporate responsibility. On the other hand, by ignoring obvious problems, this will raise doubts among investors and perhaps a red flag with the SEC.

Focus on consistency.

As with all communications, consistency is essential. In composing the shareholders letter, management should review all of its press releases and other communications made over the past year to ensure that the year-end discussion matches up with the financials and watch-points released earlier in the year. Solutions to earlier critical issues should be clarified and the reasons for changes in strategic plans should be enumerated. Displaying transparency, candor and high ethical standards builds confidence and trust. Except for providing a vision for the coming year, there should be no surprises in the shareholders letter.

Discuss Corporate Governance.

Given the developments in corporate governance (Chapter III), it is advisable for the CEO or President in the shareholders' letter to take the opportunity to express a personal commitment to high standards of corporate governance and describe the steps that the company has initiated to enhance the effectiveness of these measures within the company. Not only is this information required by law, but it is increasingly seen by investors as an indicator of commitment and trustworthiness.

Making the Best Use of the SEC Requirements: Forms 10K and 10Q

While SEC documents are largely prescribed by government regulations, management has the choice of minimally meeting the information requirements or of *including a detailed, substantive description of the company's business plan and strategy for growth.* Many companies view their SEC filings as par for the course with being a public entity. However, considering the fact that these documents are widely available as a result of online services such as Edgar, it is a mistake not to view them as an opportunity to convey a company's story and establish a basis on which the company should be valued.

The appropriate place within the SEC filing in which a company can articulate its business strategy is the Company Overview and Management Discussion and Analysis (MD&A) sections. It is here where current and potential investors look to understand what a company is all about as well as what is transpiring at a company. Indeed, the Securities Exchange Act provides that the MD&A is "intended to provide, in one section of a filing, material historical and prospective textual disclosure enabling investors and other users to assess the financial condition and results of operations of the registrant, with particular emphasis on the registrant's prospects for the future."

It is important to note that these sections are also where financial websites, including Yahoo Finance, Raging Bull and Bloomberg pick up most of the important facts on each quoted company.

Therefore, if constructed properly, the MD&A should:

• Delineate for investors and potential investors *a road map* of the company's current and potential position in its market sector,

• Provide an analysis of the competitive and risk environment,

• Discuss a company's mission and vision,

• Detail accomplishments and challenges of the past year or quarter, and

• Outline a growth strategy for the coming year.

Through these discussions, management can alert shareholders and investors to those important benchmarks or "watch points" for the next 12 months – developments that investors can keep an eye out for that will demonstrate execution and ensure a schedule of growth for the company. Here, too, is the opportunity to engender confidence with investors by talking about the important issues of corporate governance and how the company's management will be addressing these matters in the coming year. Such an in-depth discussion provides unique insight into the company that investors are eager to gain. Creating this section of the 10K enables management to clarify the company's focus and think through what has been achieved, where the company is going, and the steps needed to get there.

Of course, the SEC will scrutinize the MD&A very carefully for full and accurate disclosure and discussion of the risks as well as the potential of a company's business. In particular, there is emphasis on financial plans, capital resources, off-balance sheet transactions, revenue recognition, etc. This increased scrutiny can create anxiety in the executive suite, and sometimes may lead to less, rather than more, disclosure. However, the new requirements under the Sarbanes-Oxley Act and Regulation Fair Disclosure (see Chapter III) are and should be an impetus to enhanced communications. They present an opportunity for business executives to insist that professionals serving them provide, in plain English, a better, clearer, more accurate road map to business success. Such in-depth discussion builds confidence from all constituencies. It also provides management with a master document with clear benchmarks that every investor can follow.

Press Releases – Demonstrating execution and reinforcing success in the company's story and road map

Means of communication such as SEC filings and the annual report should present the broad picture of a company's business. With this taken care of, the next step is to "put your nose to the grindstone" and execute on the plan. As a company moves forward in doing what it says it is going to do, investors, strategic partners, major distributors, large customers and other key players will want to see regular updates on the latest developments and progress. Press releases are the appropriate tool to accomplish this.

To keep the company's value and growth story front and center, well constructed, frequent press releases – written in clear, standard English (no legalese or technology "geek-speak") – should be disseminated over the financial news wires and either emailed or faxed to investors. Each press release is an opportunity to reinforce the company's plan and add a new chapter to its story. Continuous news flow maintains investor interest and can help generate a positive investor response in the company's share price and liquidity. If a company has articulated an aggressive growth strategy and, as a result, believes it merits a higher-than-average price/earnings multiple, press releases demonstrating such growth can go a long way toward reinforcing why the company is entitled to a higher valuation.

A healthy balance must be struck between putting out too few press releases and inundating the wires with announcements that are of no value. Any news event that is material (contains information that would cause an investor to buy or sell stock) and is part of a company's business plan and story is appropriate for a press release. On the other hand, too many ancillary announcements unrelated to the road map may be perceived as promotional or touting.

The other extreme can be equally as damaging. The company that only issues quarterly earnings press releases may be perceived as sleeping at the wheel during the months between each quarter. Even if the ultimate results show progress, the fact that management has not found it important to update its investors on events taking place over a three month period may be perceived as demonstrating a lack of care to investors' desire for information. And, in any business, if management is executing successfully, at least one event takes place each quarter that is worthy of announcement.

A professional, effective press release should include the following elements as found in a press release of New York Stock Exchange listed Arbitron, Inc.:

• A dateline that includes the city and state of the company headquarters and the date (month, day, year) of the release
New York, NY, July 15, 2001

• A headline that conveys a single clear message about the news event **(bolded)**.

ARBITRON INC. ACQUIRES MARKETING RESOURCES PLUS FROM VNU

• A subheadline to identify something unique within the press release or to point out a trend in which the company has been successful (*italicized*, not bolded).

Indianapolis-Based Firm Is a Leading Provider of Media Buying
Software Systems to Local and Regional Advertising Agencies

• A first sentence that starts with the name of the company followed by its stock exchange, stock symbol and short company description.

Arbitron Inc. (NYSE: ARB) an international media and marketing research firm . . .

• A first paragraph that substantiates the headline (and sub-headline) in no more than two short sentences.

. . . announced today that it has acquired Marketing Resources Plus (MRP) from Interactive Market Systems, Inc., part of the

VNU Media Measurement & Information Group, for $8.9 million in cash.

- One or two paragraphs discussing the impact of the news on the business.

> Based in Indianapolis, Marketing Resources Plus is a leading provider of media buying software systems to local and regional advertising agencies for broadcast and print media. The company develops, markets and supports a suite of software services used by more than 800 agencies and advertisers across the United States.

- A quote from management that puts the news event in context with past news announcements and the company's business plan.

> "Marketing Resources Plus and its suite of software are a perfect complement to Arbitron and our current portfolio of software services," said Steve Morris, president and chief executive officer, Arbitron Inc. "By combining the talent and resources of both organizations, Arbitron will be better able to develop new software solutions, based on a common platform, that will give our agency and station customers a seamless, electronic buy-sell process."

> "This acquisition allows Arbitron to create new applications that combine the sophisticated multimedia buying capabilities available in

MRP's SmartPlus® with the powerful research features currently in Arbitron's TAPSCAN® and Media Professional[SM] software," said Carol Hanley, senior vice president, Advertiser/ Agency Services, Arbitron Inc. "The new systems we envision for the future will help improve the effectiveness of the millions of dollars in local market advertising that is planned and placed using MRP software."

"The local and regional agencies are ready for a breakthrough in media buying software that enables them to operate more efficiently and gives them the opportunity to differentiate themselves competitively," said Rochelle Sandberg, vice president, Client Services, Marketing Resources Plus. "This acquisition combines the resources of two businesses into a single organization that is committed to take media buying software to the next level."

- A concluding paragraph that contains the "boiler plate" – a uniform, one-paragraph description of what the company does, which is repeated consistently in all company communications. This ensures that the press and other interested parties are at all times familiar with the company's fundamental business focus. It also removes the possibility that the press and other interested parties will misrepresent what the company does for a living.

About Arbitron

Arbitron Inc. (NYSE: ARB) is an international media and marketing research firm serving radio broadcasters, cable companies, advertisers, advertising agencies and outdoor advertising companies in the United States, Mexico and Europe. Arbitron's core businesses are measuring network and local market radio audiences across the United States; surveying the retail, media and product patterns of local market consumers; and providing application software used for analyzing media audience and marketing information data. The Company is developing the Portable People Meter, a new technology for radio, television and cable ratings. Arbitron's marketing and business units are supported by a world-renowned research and technology organization located in Columbia, Maryland. Arbitron has approximately 850 full-time employees; its executive offices are located in New York City. Through its Scarborough Research joint venture with VNU, Inc., Arbitron also provides media and marketing research services to the broadcast television, cable, magazine, newspaper, outdoor, and online industries.

- The symbols "# # #" evidencing the conclusion of the press release (centered).

"# # #"

- A Safe-harbor provision (*italicized*).

> *The information contained in this press release, other than historical information, consists of forward-looking statements within the meaning of Section 27A of the Securities Act and Section 21E of the Exchange Act. These statements may involve risks and uncertainties that could cause actual results to differ materially from those described in such statements. Although the Company believes that the expectations reflected in such forward-looking statements are reasonable, it can give no assurance that such expectations will prove to have been correct. Important factors beyond the Company's control, including general economic conditions, [other risk factors relevant to a particular company] and other factors could cause actual results to differ materially from the Company's expectations.*

The All-important Quote

The most important part of the press release is the quote from management. It is here that the CEO, President, CFO or other relevant member of management can articulate the significance of the news event and put it into context with the company's business plan and growth strategy.

A press release without a quote or other explanatory statement will become an isolated event. Any investor who reads a press release without a quote will have no idea what it means to the overall company or to why the news should be considered in making an educated decision on whether or not to invest. When issuing a press release, the assumption need be made that the reader knows nothing about the company's past or what it has said about its future.

The quote is an opportunity for management to exude excitement in its business and at the same time to establish the completion of a benchmark that evidences further execution of the business plan. The quote enables investors to follow along with the company as it grows, knowing that the company remains focused.

The following quote from Lipman Electronic Engineering, a publicly traded company on the Nasdaq National Market, epitomizes how the quote provides a great opportunity to reiterate the growth strategy of a company and to put the news being announced in context with that strategy. It also demonstrates where the company is going in the near future so that investors have a better understanding of what they should be looking out for.

> Commenting on the quarter and year-end results, Isaac Angel, President and Chief Executive Officer of Lipman said, "Our financial performance for the fourth quarter and full year was extremely strong, as we achieved record revenues and profitability for the year, generated cash and maintained strong margins relative to the industry. Our results for 2003 were driven by continued acceptance of our solutions in existing markets.
>
> In addition, we have had a great deal of success in penetrating key geographic markets. We

began selling into Latin America during 2003 and sales to the region accounted for an increasing percentage of our revenues as the year progressed. We took steps toward expanding Lipman's presence in other new markets through the opening of Lipman Italia S.r.l in Milan. We continue to target new regions that will enhance Lipman's global reach going forward and are proceeding with our plan to establish a U.K. subsidiary during 2004."

"During 2003, we introduced a significant number of new products. These products include new countertop and mobile terminals and PIN pads incorporating a wide range of communications and networking technologies to meet customer needs worldwide. These new products are a result of Lipman's ongoing strategy of developing and introducing products which help reduce payment card fraud."

He concluded, "We are pleased with the success of Lipman's recent initial public offering. Our balance sheet, already strong with $57.5 million in cash and limited debt, has been further strengthened as a result of the proceeds from this IPO in the United States. Given our current market position, we believe that a tremendous opportunity exists for Lipman to expand into new countries, enhance our suite of offerings through the introduction of new products and penetrate new vertical markets. Given our combination of a globally recognized brand, leading position in a growing market, technological innovation and financial strength, we believe Lipman is well positioned to achieve its strategic goals both in the short and long term, growing our business, expanding our market share and enhancing shareholder value."

Earnings Releases

Earnings releases have somewhat different requirements, but the general principles above apply. The impact of new government legislation is extensive and is discussed in more detail in Chapter III. In addition to the general guidelines above, earnings releases must also contain the following:

- GAAP numbers proceeding pro forma numbers (pursuant to Reg G, see Chapter III)

- Comparative figures for the quarter and for the year-to-date

- Factual detail putting the financial information in context

- A quote highlighting the relevance of the financial information and setting the stage for the near future (see Lipman quote above)

- A comparative balance sheet

As is true with all press releases, consistency in format will reinforce the even more important factor of providing consistent information. Each release is a chapter in the continuing story about a company. Sudden plot twists without explanation immediately raise red flags. In preparing each release it is therefore important to look back at previous releases and to ask the question, "Is the new information consistent with what was previously said?" If not, an explanation should be provided.

The Conference Call

In this era of hyper-regulation, many executives may want to forego the quarterly earnings conference call for fear of making misstatements or opening themselves up to aggressive cross-examination. However, the conference call is a key opportunity for shareholders and potential investors to learn more about the company and the competence of management. By webcasting the call, full disclosure is accounted for under Regulation FD.

Preparation for this event is essential. Whether it is purely audio or is a visual web cast, a conference call establishes trust and confidence. It demonstrates that management is comfortable in what is going on in its business – good or bad – and understands the importance of sharing this information with its investors.

Investors, analysts and shareholders are very alert to how management responds to questions. Do the company's leaders fumble the facts and dodge hard questions? Or do they tell the company's story clearly and consistently, despite tough questions that may be asked. It is necessary therefore to contemplate all possible questions that may be asked during the question and answer session of the conference call. (While the author of this book does not condone paying attention to the chat rooms of the financial websites, they are a good place to understand and learn what questions and issues may be relevant to investors.)

If the company's top brass demonstrates command of the facts, articulates a clear vision of the company's future, puts forth a plan to confront new challenges, and confidently discusses the company's current financials, whether positive or negative, such frankness and assertiveness will inspire a new level of trust among all stakeholders. Learning to manage this important communications tool is a hallmark of leadership that investors are looking for.

SECTION B: MAKING THE STORY CLEAR AND CONCISE

The Fact Sheet – Sharpening the Message for Maximum Impact

The major documents of the 10K and the Annual Report become the foundation for a much shorter, highly condensed document that serves as possibly the best print communicator of a company's value – the two-page Fact Sheet. Succinct and focused, it is designed to present the company's investment potential as concisely and forcefully as possible at a glance. Having written the long, legally and financially complex business plan and strategy, management can now boil down all information to six major points:

1. An *Overview* of the company's business – what the company does for a living.

2. A checklist of five or six "*Investment Considerations*" – the unique strengths and outstanding competitive advantages that set forth why the company is worthy of an investment.

3. A summary of *growth strategy* – every company has one or should.

4.   Recent *financial results* and *current stock information*, using charts and graphs whenever possible.

5.   *News headlines* from recent press releases.

6.   A one-paragraph *industry overview* or *competitive analysis*.

An example of a small-capitalization company that presents its complete story in a concise and interesting fashion can be found in that of American Stock Exchange listed Path 1 Network Technologies.

CORPORATE PROFILE

Path 1 Network Technologies Inc.

Path 1 Network Technologies Inc. is engaged in the development and supply of products that enable the transportation and distribution of real-time, broadcast-quality video over Internet protocol (IP) networks. The Company's products are used in two customer segments of the video market: cable companies that supply video and other on-demand services, and network providers that transmit real-time video to one or more locations throughout the United States or the world (long-haul transmission). Path 1's customers include cable, broadcast and satellite companies, movie studios, carriers and government and educational institutions. The Company works with several business partners, including Scientific Atlanta, Inc., as resellers of its product lines.

Path 1 Solutions

By enabling the transportation and distribution of real-time, high-quality video over existing IP networks, Path 1 products provide significant benefits to those with a need to distribute video. This method of transmission offers greater feasibility, efficiency, content on demand, decreased capital and operations costs, customization and flexibility.

Long Haul Customers

The ability for long haul customers to send video over existing IP networks significantly reduces the current need of these providers to rent dedicated high bandwidth connections to service the specified locations. Aside from providing a cost advantage, Path 1 products enable customers increased flexibility in terms of where and when the video is transmitted. Long Haul customers include: **DreamWorks LLC, C-span, PanAmSat, RTVi, Level (3), and Wiltel/Vyvx.**

Cable Company Customers

The Chameleon vidX product line has been specifically developed for cable companies to use existing digital set-top boxes already in consumer homes to provide video-on-demand services. The more efficient use of bandwidth allows cable companies to increase the volume of content available for delivery whenever requested by the cable subscriber, or to increase the number of subscribers with existing content volume. Additionally, Path 1 products provide cable companies with flexibility to deliver high definition television, which could potentially overwhelm the bandwidth capacity of current delivery technologies. Cable customers include **Time-Warner** and **Cablevision.**

Competitive Advantages

- Offers the only coast-to-coast tried and proven broadcast video over IP networking solution.

- Products allow customers to employ existing infrastructure to transmit video content using IP communications networks; allows for lowered costs and permits greater flexibility in the delivery of video content.

- Unique technology focused on network-processor-based architecture allows for faster product development and reduces development and production costs.

- Path 1 products provide the fastest video-over-IP solution available today: capable of transmitting up to 270 Mbps of uncompressed video.

- Path 1 products offer broadcasters the ability to "future proof" their communications network with live video over IP gateways by using the Company's unique software-driven architecture to ensure scalability and upgradeability.

- Securely positioned to support the evolution of broadcasting as cable companies aggressively seek products that can be easily integrated into existing networks in order to provide consumers with the additional types of content-on-demand.

Management

Frederick A. Cary....CEO, President, Director
Ronald O. Fellman...Founder, Chief Technology Officer
David Carnevale.....VP, Sales & Marketing
John Zavoli...........CFO, General Counsel, Corp Sec.
Patrick C. Bohana...VP & General Manager

Financial Highlights

Exchange:	AMEX
Ticker:	PNO
Price (11/5/03):	$5.10
Market Cap:	$27.97M
52-week high:	$9.60
52-week low:	$3.00
Shares outstanding:	5.43M
Float:	4.60M
Fiscal year end:	December

Path 1 Products

Path 1 products take the form of custom boards, boxes and software. All of the products adhere to applicable open standards to be interoperable with other telecommunications equipment and offer flexible and cost-effective solutions. Any Path 1 product may be produced "Private Label".

Chameleon vidX™ Product Family
(Chameleon vidX™ DemuX and Chameleon vidX™ MuX)
Supports Video on Demand (VoD) and HDTV applications while significantly reducing capital expenditure and extending the useful life of cable operators' core networks.

Cx1000 IP Video Gateways
Specifically designed to meet the stringent requirement of broadcasters for transporting real-time broadcast-quality video, uncompressed or compressed, over existing IP networks.

Cx1410-IP Video Multiplexer
Designed to bridge the IP-based optical-fiber network with the QAM-based Hybrid Fiber Coax (HFC) distribution network for Video on Demand (VOD) Applications.

Growth Strategy

Path 1 is focused on the expansion of its three main revenue sources, product sales, contract services and license revenues.

Product Sales: Path 1's strategy is to aggressively pursue resources that introduce the Company's products to the market. Strategic relationships with major equipment and content providers, along with building a direct sales and marketing staff within the Company will remain the over-riding driver for continued product sales.

Contract Services: The Company's development of its integrated QAM product with its partner, Aurora Networks, will pave the way for a continued stream of contract service revenues.....................

License Revenues: The License revenue stream will contribute strongly to the Company's revenues as most of the product's new features and upgrades can be uploaded to installed equipment by using software, demonstrating to customers that Path 1 products are upgradeable and scalable by acquiring a software upload.

Path 1 is also focused on the continuous launch and marketing of new products. Product development is based on customer requirements for increased performance, flexibility and functionality.

Selected Financial Information	In Thousands	
	Quarter Ended	
	9/30/03	9/30/02
Total Revenues	$787	$832
Gross Profit	$288	$301
Net Loss	$(2,666)	$(1,297)
Net Loss per common share	$(0.59)	$(0.91)

Investment Considerations

- Strengthened balance sheet supports strategic business development; recent public offering of $15.5 million of common stock and warrants increased cash position to more than $10 million at close of 3rd quarter 2003.

- Strongly positioned in IP video market as the Company specializes in video transmission that supports both broadcast television and video-on-demand.

- Opportunity for long-term growth as cable companies continuously look toward supplying customers with enhanced Video-on-Demand services.

- Established partnerships, including Scientific-Atlanta Inc., supporting Path1's enhanced presence among large MSO customers.

- Growing list of customers including leading cable companies, such as Time-Warner and Cablevision.

- 3rd Quarter 2003 net revenue increased sequentially by 10% to $787,000 over 2nd Quarter revenue of $714,000.

- Product sales revenue increased 9% to 2% to $87,000 from $537,000 for the three months ended September 30, 2003 and 2002, respectively, and over 150% sequentially from $226,000 in the 2nd Quarter of 2003.

Recent News

Nov 17, 2003...Path 1 Network Technologies Clarifies Form S-3 Filing

Nov 12, 2003...Path 1 Network Technologies Selects Townsend Inc. for Integrated Marketing Services

Nov 11, 2003...Path 1 Network Technologies Announces 3rd Quarter Results

Nov 10, 2003...Path 1 Showcases Video-Over-IP Solution at Society of Motion Picture and Television Engineers Conference

Nov 6, 2003....Path 1 Network Technologies Inc. to Present at Westergaard Small-Cap Conference

Company Contact

6215 Ferris Square #140
San Diego, CA 92121
Phone: 858-450-4220
Fax: 858-450-4203
Toll Free: 877-ONE-PATH
www.path1.com

The Investment Considerations

The most important part of the fact sheet is the section that provides the investment considerations. These key pieces of information answer the very basic question, *"Why should I invest?"* The investment considerations for the undervalued company provide the information necessary for the value investor to answer this question. For the growth investor, the investment considerations make the point on how the company intends to grow at a rate faster than other companies in the industry and those activities that demonstrate that the company is in fact doing so.

Examples of compelling investment considerations for companies in virtually any industry can include several of the following:

Financial investment considerations

• $350 + million current annual sales run rate; sales for the second quarter amounted to $8.7 million representing a 34.1% increase over the comparable period in 2002.

• Net income for fiscal 2003 increased to $19.2 million from $1.3 million reported in fiscal 2002.

• Strong financial position -- $106.5 million in cash and liquid investments; no corporate debt; 2003 dividend of $0.04 per share; operating cash flow of $25.6 million in first six months of 2003.

• Earnings per share have increased by double digits for the past 10 years.

• Return on equity increases to 11.6% from 6.8% in 1998 while book value has increased to $24.79.

• Company is currently traded at a discount to Net Asset Value.

• Current backlog and quality pipeline of approximately $35 million and a contract pipeline of business opportunities in excess of $200 million.

• Company's board has authorized the repurchase of 278,771 shares, or approximately 5% of the company's shares of common stock as of September 30, 2002.

Industry investment considerations

• A sizeable market opportunity exists – industry spending was $14.1 billion in 2002 and is expected to reach about $36.2 billion in 2004, representing a compound annual growth rate of 60.2%.

• The company has exceeded the industry average for Return on Equity over the past three years and continues to outperform the S&P 500.

• Company continuously outperforms competitors – company beat the industry in 2002 by more than 27%.

• Senior management is composed of world-renowned industry experts.

- The company has consistently increased its annual dividend for the past 28 years and pays one of the highest dividend yields in the industry.

Guidance/growth driven investment considerations

- Company's stated goal is to grow its revenue base from its current annual run rate of $30 million to $100 million in the next five years.

- Expansion of product lines through acquisitions that complement existing products that are focused on high-value, high-niche products with minimal direct competition.

- The company has a successful track record of acquisition-driven growth and currently pursues an acquisition strategy aimed at higher-growth markets.

- Strong projected revenue growth of $7-8 million in 2003, indicating a 105% increase from 2002.

- Company expects revenue of approximately $25.35 million for 2004 with income from operations of approximately $3.75 million, or approximately $0.31 per diluted share.

Business Plan investment considerations

- Company has implemented cost reduction and cost containment measures to help obtain profitability.

•   Strategic plan to strengthen corporate infrastructure, including facilities, product and personnel, is expected to provide strong growth for 2004.

•   Margins expanding as a result of the company's shift to a more direct marketing strategy.

•   Recent acquisition of a 119,000 square foot distribution facility is expected to expand company's production capacity to up to $200 million in annual sales.

By selecting from the above list several investment considerations and updating the fact sheet at least quarterly, any interested investor will have sufficient information on which to make an educated determination on whether or not to invest. These considerations also form the basis for a company's investor presentation.

The Corporate/Investor Presentation

> *"Thank you for taking the time to meet with me today and giving me the opportunity to present to you the story of Acme Corporation. Before I begin, I would like to give you a brief overview of who we are at Acme Corporation and why we believe Acme Corporation is worthy of your investment . . .*

*   *   *

> *. . . and, in conclusion, let me reiterate why we hope you will invest in Acme Corporation . . ."*

Another succinct document that communicates a company's story and investment proposition, both through print and visual presentation, is the company's PowerPoint investor presentation. The content of this presentation is a variation on the Fact Sheet, and the information must, of course, be consistent with all other company documents and materials. In particular, the investment considerations contained in the fact sheet are the same as those contained in the investor presentation and, as seen in the opening remarks above by Acme Corporation's management, serve as both an introduction and conclusion to the Acme Corporation story.

The investor presentation is typically given in a one-on-one or group setting. Therefore, the presenter must consider the audience in which he or she is presenting to and conform the presentation to the specific needs of the individual investor.

It is important to keep in mind, however, that some investors may not have the benefit of commentary by management. As discussed below, it is recommended that the investor presentation be made part of a company's investor kit or package since, like the fact sheet, it tells a company's story in a succinct and efficient manner. To the extent the presentation exists as a stand-alone document without the benefit of management commentary, each slide must therefore have an intended point and provide sufficient information for the viewer to reach the conclusion intended by the company without the benefit of having management available to answer questions.

The following presentation of Nasdaq listed Bakers Footwear sets forth those slides and an appropriate order for best communicating a company's story and investment proposition:

- Safe harbor clause

Safe Harbor Statement

This presentation contains forward-looking statements that are based on information currently available to us and are subject to a number of risks, uncertainties and other factors that could cause our actual results, performance, prospects or opportunities in the remainder of fiscal year 2004 and beyond to differ materially from those expressed in, or implied by these statements. These risks, uncertainties and other factors include, among other things, the unpredictability of future revenues and cash flow, intense competition, and risks associated with consumer preferences and trends and management of growth. More information about factors that potentially could affect Bakers' results, performance, prospects and opportunities are included in the Company's amended S-1 filing dated January 20, 2004.

2

- Clear, comprehensive overview of the company

Bakers Footwear Group

Bakers is the leading specialty retailer of moderately-priced fashion footwear to young women

4

- Company mission statement (optional)

- Investment considerations

Investment Highlights

- Dominant market position focused on attractive demographic niche

- Strong unit economics

- Significant growth opportunities while leveraging existing infrastructure

- Disciplined management approach

- Excellent sourcing capabilities

- Advanced information systems

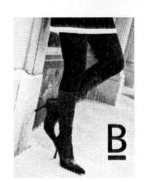

5

- Industry overview

The Women's Footwear Market

$19.2 Billion in 2002

Discounters
35%

Specialty Stores
40%

Department Stores
25%

Source: Market size estimate from The NPD Group, Inc.; percentages from Company estimates.

10

- Key customers or partners

Attractive Customer Base

- Young women ages 12-29

  - *Attractive demographic*
    - The largest US female consumer group (approximately 38 million in 2000 [1])

  - *Image conscious*
    - Embraces fashion trends, tends to purchase multiple pairs
    - Cares about how she looks and spends a lot on her wardrobe

  - *Relatively high disposable income*
    - Spends an average of $234 per year on footwear [2]

  - *Shops in malls*
    - Enjoys social atmosphere
    - It's where she buys her apparel

Sources: [1] U.S. Census Bureau's 2000 Census
         [2] U.S. Bureau of Labor Statistics

11

- Growth Strategy

Open New Stores in Key Locations

- Identified over 200 key locations
  - 15 new stores by the end of FY 2004
  - 35 more by the end of FY 2005
  - Focus on fashion markets and malls
  - Leverage existing infrastructure
  - New stores are profitable in first operating quarter

- Capitalize on market opportunities
  - 8 stores acquired in 2001
  - 33 stores acquired in 2002
  - Less capital investment required

21

- Growth Strategy (con't.)

Expand Presence of New Format Stores

- Distinctive, upscale and contemporary look
  - Highly visible locations in high-traffic malls

- 32 existing stores remodeled into new format
  - Sales increases of 15% (where location has not changed)
  - Identified an additional 80 stores to be remodeled
  - Remodels coincide with lease renewals

- 9 new format stores built since 2001 (open at least 12 months)
  - Average annual sales of $741,000; cash flow of $91,000+

- Currently operate 36 new format stores (open at least 12 months)
  - Average annual sales of $889,000; cash flow of $132,000

- More than half of all stores expected to be new format by end of 2005

23

Increase Same Store Sales

- Capitalize on current fashion trends

- Increase the sale of branded footwear and accessories
  - Increased price points
  - Higher gross margin $
  - Increased traffic and customer loyalty

24

Additional slides demonstrating a growth strategy may include new or growing markets, expanding distribution channels, potential new customers or new strategic partnerships.

- Financials

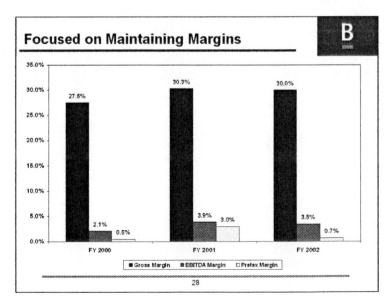

Historical Operating Results

($ in millions)	Fiscal Year			
	2000 [1]	2001 [2]	2002 [3]	2003 [4]
Net Sales	$ 140.7	$ 140.8	$ 150.6	$ 147.0
Gross Profit	38.7	42.6	45.1	N/A
Gross Margin	*27.5%*	*30.3%*	*30.0%*	*N/A*
EBITDA	2.9	6.7	5.2	N/A
EBITDA Margin	*2.1%*	*4.7%*	*3.5%*	*N/A*
Proforma Pretax Income	0.7	4.2	1.1	N/A
Pretax Margin	*0.5%*	*3.0%*	*0.7%*	*N/A*
Pro Forma Net Income	0.4	2.6	0.6	N/A
Number of Stores at End of Year	209	202	233	215

(1) Includes $1.0 million gain on lease termination and $1.2 million loss on debt extinguishment
Excludes $1.1 million amortization of negative goodwill
(2) FY 2001 is a 53 week period
Excludes $1.1 million amortization of negative goodwill
(3) Excludes $1.7 million write-off of deferred IPO costs
Excludes $2.8 million cumulative effect of change in accounting due to write-off of negative goodwill
(4) FY 2003 results are unaudited and subject to adjustment

27

Focused on Maintaining Margins

FY 2000: Gross Margin 27.5%, EBITDA Margin 2.1%, Pretax Margin 0.5%
FY 2001: Gross Margin 30.3%, EBITDA Margin 3.9%, Pretax Margin 3.0%
FY 2002: Gross Margin 30.0%, EBITDA Margin 3.5%, Pretax Margin 0.7%

Legend: ■ Gross Margin ■ EBITDA Margin ☐ Pretax Margin

28

- Financials (con't.)

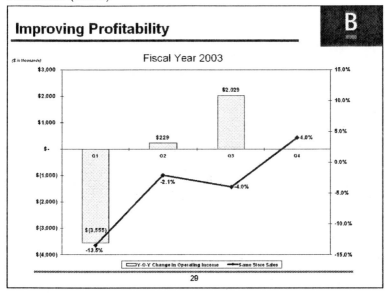

Improving Profitability

B

($ in thousands)

Fiscal Year 2003

Chart showing Y-O-Y Change in Operating Income (bars) and Same Store Sales (line):

Quarter	Y-O-Y Change in Operating Income	Same Store Sales
Q1	$(3,555)	-13.5%
Q2	$229	-2.1%
Q3	$2,029	-4.0%
Q4		4.0%

Legend: Y-O-Y Change in Operating Income — Same Store Sales

29

Pro Forma Balance Sheet

B

	October 4, 2003 [1]
Current Assets	
Cash and cash equivalents	$ 369,150
Accounts receivable and other receivables	983,292
Inventories	16,880,701
Deferred tax assets	974,200
Other current assets	891,579
Total Current Assets	20,098,922
Property and equipment, net	13,041,656
Noncurrent deferred tax assets	48,013
Other assets	139,000
Total Assets	**$ 33,327,591**
Current Liabilities	
Accounts payable and accrued expenses	$ 8,913,436
Revolving credit agreement	4,011,097
Current maturities of subordinated debt and capital lease obligations	1,137,490
Total Current Liabilities	14,062,023
Subordinated debt, less current maturities	251,872
Obligations under capital leases, less current maturities	1,555,314
Other liabilities	1,168,156
Shareholders' Equity	
Common stock, $.0001 par value	437
Deferred stock compensation	(2,990)
Additional paid-in capital	16,292,579
Retained earnings	-
Total Shareholders' Equity	16,290,226
Total Liabilities and Shareholders' Equity	**$ 33,327,591**

(1) Pro forma for offering of 1,750,000 shares and application of proceeds
Excludes 262,500 shares issuable upon the exercise of the underwriters' over-allotment option

31

- Competitive positioning and advantages

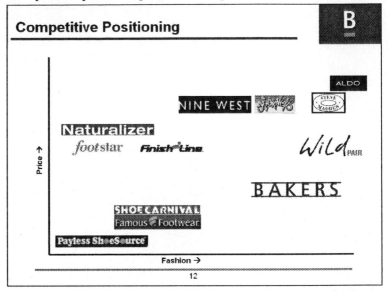

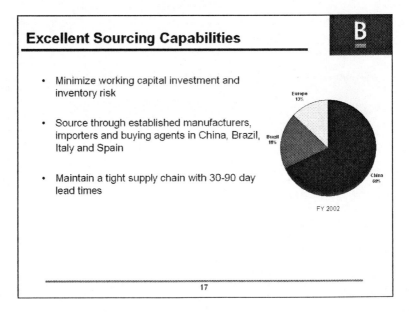

- Competitive positioning and advantages (con't.)

Advanced Information Systems

- Fully integrated, scalable, cost-effective systems in place

- Enable management to keep fast moving inventory in stock, minimize shrinkage and reduce markdowns

- Timely decision making tools
  - JDA Software enterprise retail solution
    - Inventory and back office management
  - Arthur Allocation
    - Merchandise allocation
  - XBR Proact POS technology suite
    - Loss prevention
    - Sales & productivity optimizer
    - Audit/data control
  - MarketMax
    - Assortment planning

18

Disciplined Management Approach

- Management decisions are supported by extensive data, systems and tools
  - Facilitated rapid response to changes in consumer demand over the last 18 months
  - Reduced inventory commitments, controlled excess inventory

- Streamlined operating infrastructure
  - Freight
  - Shrinkage
  - Store payroll
  - Marketing

- Management structure has positioned Bakers for profitable growth

19

- Management team

Experienced Management Team

Name/Title	Prior Employers	Experience
Peter A. Edison – Chairman and CEO	• Edison Footwear Group *(500 stores)* • Edison Big & Tall • Chandlers/Sacha of London	26 years
Michele A. Bergerac – President and Chief Merchant	• Edison Footwear Group *(500 stores)* • May Company (incl. G. Fox and Foley's) • Abraham & Strauss	26 years
Lawrence L. Spanley – CFO, Treasurer and Secretary	• Senack Shoes (division of Interco)	30 years
Stanley K. Tusman – EVP – Inventory Management & Information Systems	• Edison Footwear Group *(500 stores)* • Genesco *(500 stores)* • Claire's Boutiques *(400 stores)* • Limited *(350 stores)*	30 years
Mark D. Ianni – EVP – General Merchandise Manager	• Edison Footwear Group *(500 stores)*	23 years
Joseph R. Vander Pluym – EVP – Store Operations	• Edison Footwear Group *(500 stores)* • Lucky Brand Apparel Stores *(80 stores)* • Merry-Go-Round *(700 stores)*	29 years

9

- Reprise of investment considerations as a means to summarize the presentation.

Summary

- Dominant market position
- Experienced management team
- Strong results
- Poised for growth

33

For the company that is positioning itself as representing a value opportunity, messages to emphasize should include the company's peer group and an analysis of competitive financial information (e.g. P/E ratios) of the peer group.   Depending on a company's business or industry, additional slides may be required. For example, for companies in the precious metals industry, slides pertaining to the different mines and the stages of production are important.   For biotech companies, slides dealing with the various stages of FDA approval are necessary. For manufacturing companies, investors will want to learn about the company's facilities and manufacturing capacity.

Regardless of a company's industry, the above slides provide an appropriate template in which to get started. Management should figure that it will have between 20 and 30 minutes in which to make their entire presentation.   It is therefore necessary that the investor presentation be kept to no more than 20 slides in total.

The Investor Relations Kit – Pulling the Communications Platform Together

The investor package or kit tells the complete story of a company. It is the face that a company wishes to present of itself. If it comes neatly and professionally presented, the initial reaction is that the company is buttoned-up and treats its investor relations in a serious and professional manner.   If pages from a company's 10Q are missing or are stapled upside-down, that company will be viewed as sloppy. If a company does not possess an investor package, that company has lost the ability to dictate and control who it is and what it represents.   It is therefore essential that a company spend time compiling those materials that will provide investors with sufficient information in which to understand the company and make an informed investment decision.

A comprehensive investor kit should contain all essential IR materials, including:

- The company's most recent annual report

- The fact sheet

- SEC filings (most recent 10K, 10Q and Proxy statement)

- Press releases from prior six months

- Investor presentation

- Fax/email list request card

- Marketing brochures where appropriate

- Industry or financial media clippings

Companies are dissuaded from including financial research reports in their investor packages. The reason for this is that investors view such inclusions as touting or promoting of a company's stock since most companies that include such reports only include those that are positive. (Would a company really include in its investor package a research report that recommended that investors sell?) Moreover, distributing research reports suggests that a company endorses all information contained in the report. To the extent an investor is a client of an investment bank or research firm, they can subscribe to that firm's research and choose which recommendations to pay attention to.

In its investor kit, the company should provide factual, unbiased and complete information that will allow investors to reach their own

conclusion on whether or not to invest. If a company is fortunate to have research coverage and investment banking support, a preferred alternative to informing investors of the coverage that exists is to include in the investor package a one-page piece of paper specifying the analysts that follow the company and providing the analysts' contact information.

3

The IR Website & Communicating Successfully Under Sarbanes-Oxley and the New SEC Regulations

The Sarbanes-Oxley Act and new SEC regulations, instituted following the corporate scandals of 2002, have put many new restrictions and requirements on how companies communicate their financial information to the public, investors and potential investors. There has been much discussion and debate on the extent to which these rules require companies to institute new internal procedures and create time-consuming new documents, all of which require significant financial expenditure. Notwithstanding the burdens they impose (particularly the financial burdens), Sarbanes-Oxley should be viewed as an opportunity for companies to become more forthright in their communications and to enhance their value in doing so.

This Chapter takes a succinct look at the Sarbanes-Oxley Act and two of the most important new SEC requirements arising out of SOx – new Item 12 to Form 8-K and Regulation G. It also examines the impact of the new regulations on the company website and provides guidelines on what information a company needs to provide in the investor relations section, to be in compliance with the rules' mandates.

New Governance Regulations

On July 30, 2002, President Bush signed into law the Sarbanes-Oxley Act of 2002 the purpose of which was to respond to mounting concern over the increasing number of corporate scandals and frauds being perpetrated by the management teams of publicly traded companies. At its essence, Sarbanes-Oxley requires the CEO and the CFO of a company to take responsibility for internal financial reporting procedures and to certify personally all reports containing financial statements filed with the SEC.

Generally speaking, SEC regulations imposed in 2003 to implement the Sarbanes-Oxley Act accelerate filing deadlines and require fuller and more frequent disclosure of financial information. Such disclosure enhances that which was required by the SEC in Regulation Fair Disclosure (Reg FD). Reg FD was imposed by the SEC in 2000 in response to apparent selective disclosure of material information by the management teams of publicly traded companies to financial analysts and, in turn, to institutional investors who were clients of the investment banks for whom the analysts were employed. As a result, individual and retail investors were often excluded from knowledge of this information and therefore were not given the same opportunity to invest (or sell) in a company based on information provided by the companies to the analysts and institutions. Sarbanes-Oxley, for all intents and purposes, codifies many of Reg FD's requirements. It provides:

Each issuer . . . shall disclose to the public on a rapid and current basis such additional information concerning material changes in the financial condition or operation of the issuer.

Not surprisingly, in response to the Sarbanes-Oxley, some executives responded by reducing communications because of the extra time and thought required as well as the fear aroused because of the personal responsibility now imposed or because of the concern over what might happen if they unknowingly misspoke and violated some part of the rules. Other executives, however, saw the new regulations as an opportunity to communicate more fully with shareholders and, by doing so, to enhance their relationships with their shareholders and ultimately the value of their companies.

It has been suggested that 75 percent of a company's value is predicated on objective financial information such as revenues and earnings. The remaining 25 percent is based on trust and confidence in management. Recent research by Standard & Poors indicates that investors increasingly take governance practices into consideration when evaluating investment opportunities. Indeed, according to an investor survey conducted by McKinsey & Co. in 2002, it was found that almost two-thirds of investors say that governance considerations may sway their decision on whether or not to invest in a particular company. The survey also noted that 80 percent of those investors polled said they would pay a premium for well-governed companies.

The way in which a company complies with and communicates in light of the new regulations is therefore critical to its valuation. If a business and its growth strategy are truly based on sound financial information and principles, it stands to reason that the company is more likely to succeed. Therefore, communicating a company's financial controls and responsibility can only enhance the company's perceived value. Shareholders and investors will recognize not only good governance but also good business practices that ensure a sustainable bottom line. And when difficulties arise, open communication continues to earn trust and helps maintain investor confidence in the company's underlying value.

The Sarbanes-Oxley Act: Selected Highlights

Among the many matters of corporate governance and executive financial responsibility addressed by The Sarbanes-Oxley Act of July 2002 are the following key points:

> *New internal controls:*   Section 302 of Sarbanes-Oxley mandates frequent disclosure of material information affecting or likely to affect a company's financial performance.   It makes the CEO and the CFO responsible for designing internal controls, maintaining oversight, evaluating the controls' effectiveness, and reporting on these responsibilities in the company's Annual Report.

> *Code of ethics:*   A company must disclose whether it has instituted a code of ethics and if not, why it has not.   It must also promptly disclose any amendments to or waivers from this code.

> *Disclosure Committee:*   Based on the spirit of Sarbanes-Oxley, companies are recommended to form a Disclosure Committee to review filings and earnings releases, review the company's disclosure policy, and establish and monitor internal control processes for filing certifications.

> *Off-balance sheet entities:*   If a company has material off-balance sheet transactions, it must disclose what they are and how they impact the company's business in each annual and quarterly report.   The aim is not to ban such

structures but to help investors understand how a company uses them.

In summarizing its implementation of Sarbanes-Oxley, the SEC said:

> As directed by the Sarbanes-Oxley Act of 2002, we are adopting new rules and amendments to address public companies' disclosure or release of certain financial information that is calculated and presented on the basis of methodologies other than in accordance with generally accepted accounting principles (GAAP). We are adopting a new disclosure regulation, Regulation G, which will require public companies that disclose or release such non-GAAP financial measures to include, in that disclosure or release, a presentation of the most directly comparable GAAP financial measure and a reconciliation of the disclosed non-GAAP financial measure to the most directly comparable GAAP financial measure.

* * *

> Finally, we are adopting amendments that require registrants to furnish to the Commission, on Form-8K, earnings releases or similar announcements.

Therefore, in addition to the governance regulations listed above, sections of the Sarbanes-Oxley Act impact earnings release practices and the use of non-GAAP financial measures in earning releases and other public disclosures. To implement these new requirements, the SEC adopted Regulation G which governs the use of non-GAAP financial measures, such as EBITDA, income before one-time charges, and other unusual and one-time events that do not bear on a company's overall operations and ultimate earnings success as well as the new "Item 12 to Form 8-K" governing earnings releases.

Regulation G: The SEC's new Regulation G provides the framework for including financial information in earnings releases that do not conform to GAAP. The SEC has defined non-GAAP financial measures to be a numerical measure of a registrant's historical or future financial performance, financial position or cash flow that excludes or includes amounts or is subject to adjustments that have the effect of excluding amounts that are included in the most directly comparable measure calculated and presented in accordance with GAAP in the statement of income, balance sheet or statement of cash flows.

Important provisions of Regulation G include (but are not limited to):

- Regulation G includes the general disclosure requirement that a registrant, or person acting on its behalf, shall not make public a non-GAAP financial measure that, taken together with the information accompanying that measure, contains an untrue statement of a material fact or omits to state a material fact necessary in order to make the presentation of the non-GAAP financial measure, in light of the circumstances under which it is presented, not misleading.

- For any public disclosure of a non-GAAP financial measure, companies must present the most directly comparable GAAP-based measure along with reconciliation between the two figures.

- GAAP numbers must be given prominence over non-GAAP numbers.

- Non-GAAP numbers cannot exclude charges or liabilities that would be included in comparable GAAP numbers.

- Non-GAAP numbers cannot include charges or liabilities that would be excluded from comparable GAAP numbers.

- Non-GAAP numbers cannot have titles the same as or similar to GAAP titles. For example, a non-GAAP title of "operating earnings" may not be used because it can be confused with "operating income."

- If non-GAAP numbers are used, the company must explain why they are important to understanding the company.

Prior to Regulation G, it was easier to report only good news and downplay the negative. It was not atypical for a company to state in that main text of its earnings release that *"Operating earnings per share (diluted) increased 27% to $3.48 from last year's $2.59, excluding special charges and acquisition-related amortization costs."* And then, only at the bottom of the last financial table of the release did the company reveal that, according to GAAP numbers, the company earned only $1.25 per share.

Such obfuscations hardly conveyed true value and certainly did not enhance investor confidence. In light of Regulation G, companies are now required to work hard to restore public trust in the quality of financial reporting. And, many companies are successfully doing so. While some companies have discarded non-GAAP earnings entirely, the new ruling is not intended to eliminate non-GAAP measures. Its goal is simply to increase the transparency of earnings announcements by requiring companies to explain how non-GAAP figures are calculated and why they are useful.

One company recently identified its non-GAAP measures in its earnings release and qualified the use of non-GAAP numbers by stating:

> "These measures represent important internal measures of performance. Accordingly, where these non-GAAP measures are provided, it is done so that investors have the same financial data that management uses with the belief that it will assist the investment community in properly assessing the underlying performance of the company on a year-over-year and quarter-sequential basis."

The company then went on to describe in detail how each measure was useful. While such explanation appears to require significant work, it requires no more effort than past practices of creating inflated and misleading categories and figures.

It is important to note that Regulation G, while applying to any entity that is required to file pursuant to Setions 13 (a) or 15 (d) of the Exchange Act (other than a registered investment company), do not always apply to foreign private issuers. Nevertheless, if a foreign issuer desires to take advantage of the capital markets of the United States, it is strongly recommended that such a foreign issuer comply with Regulation G and all that has emanated from Sarbanes-Oxley. The reason for this is not to impose additional requirements on the foreign issuer. Rather, as stated above, it is to establish the trust and confidence necessary to achieve the additional value stemming from increased disclosure and candor.

Form 8-K: Sarbanes-Oxley seeks to ensure that earnings and financial data, and any other non-public material information regarding the company's operations, are disclosed promptly and fully. To implement this, the SEC added a new "Item 12" thereby amending Form 8-K to now require "Disclosure of Results of Operations and Financial Condition." This calls for not only disseminating press and earnings releases through a major wire service, but also filing them as exhibits to the Form 8-K. The same is true of texts of verbal public announcements and presentations that provide non-public information likely to influence investment considerations.

Effective August 23, 2004, in addition to press releases regarding the disclosure of results of operations and financial condition, additional new disclosure items must be filed as exhibits to the Form 8-K. They include non-public information regarding the:

- entry into a material agreement not made in the ordinary course of business;

- termination of a material agreement not made in the ordinary course of business;
- creation of a material, direct financial obligation or a material obligation under an off-balance sheet arrangement;

- triggering events that accelerate or increase a material, direct financial obligation or a material obligation under an off-balance sheet arrangement;

- material costs associated with exit or disposal activities;

- material impairments;

- non-reliance on previously issued financial statements or a related audit report or completed interim review (restatements); and

- notice of delisting or failure to satisfy a continued listing rule or standard, or transfer of listing.

In addition, whereas companies previously were required in their annual and quarterly reports to disclose unregistered sales of equity securities by the company and material modifications to the rights of holders of the company's securities, these requirements now also must be filed with the Form 8-K.

All must be filed *within four business days* of the initial release or other event requiring a public disclosure.

It is important to note that new Item 12 does not require that companies issue earnings releases. However, if they do, then the requirements of Item 12 apply.

Moreover, new Item 12 applies regardless of whether the press release or announcement includes disclosure of a non-GAAP financial measure.

* * *

Sarbanes-Oxley, Regulation Fair Disclosure and Regulation G are not going away any time soon. Therefore it is strongly recommended that companies view the new rules as an opportunity to communicate more fully with shareholders and others. If senior executives can embrace the new rules and communicate a willingness to be open in providing their financial information, they will increase investor confidence in their numbers and ensure a truer valuation for their companies.

The Company Website and the New Regulations

In this day of heightened investor skepticism and mistrust (and in light of Sarbanes-Oxley), the corporate website is typically the first place an investor will turn in order to learn about a company. It is the corporate website where first impressions are made. It is here where an investor will look to learn about a company and its financials, get a flavor for how a company presents itself and also learn how management views the importance of investor relations and providing that information which investors view as important.

Before contacting a company and requesting a face-to-face meeting, most investors will approach the company's website hoping that they can obtain all necessary information. Accordingly, the investor relations section of a company's website should contain all elements of its communications platform. More important, the IR section should be easily navigable and located (a tab on the home page entitled "investor relations"). Simply put, by bringing together all investor related materials in one section of a company's website – and ensuring that that section is kept up to date – a company can greatly facilitate communication with the financial community, enabling its members to more easily and fully understand the company's true strengths and value.

An effective investor relations website should include the following elements:

- Updated company fact sheet

- Investor PowerPoint presentation

- Up-to-date financial information, including all SEC documents: 10-K, 10-Q and 8-K in downloadable format

- Stock quote and other relevant financial highlights (e.g. market capitalization, daily volume, etc.)

- All press releases catalogued by year and date

- Annual report in PDF format

- Calendar of events

- Frequently asked questions

- Management bios

- All materials contained in the investor kit and communications platform downloadable in PDF format

- An interactive portion where investors can request to be added to a company's email, fax or mailing lists

- An interactive portion where investors can request to meet with management.

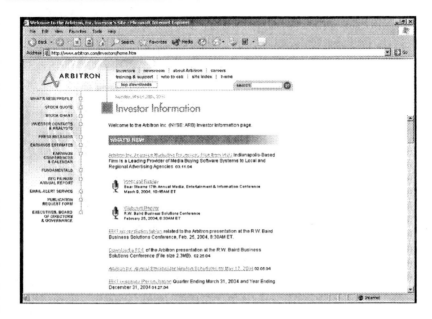

To the extent a company did not view its website as being of such importance, the new requirements of Sarbanes-Oxley now make it essential for companies to maintain such an investor relations section to their website that can promptly transmit the necessary information. Moreover, given the new requirements on internal controls, codes of ethics and disclosure policies, the IR section of a company's website provides an easy way for companies to demonstrate their compliance with Sarbanes-Oxley.

By following the template for the ideal investor relations website discussed above, a company is well on its way to complying with the new regulations. For example, an important element of the IR section of a company's website is the link that provides access to a company's SEC filings. By having such a link, a company immediately is in compliance with Sarbanes-Oxley, as it requires a company to provide access to their Forms 10-K, 10-Q and 8-K as soon as possible (and free of charge) after those reports have been filed with the SEC. If these documents are not available on the website, the company will need to explain why. It is important to note that the SEC *expects* these filings to be obtainable from the IR portion of a company's website.

To demonstrate compliance with the demands of Sarbanes-Oxley and the new SEC regulations (as well as to show investors that the company takes its corporate governance seriously), every company should have an additional section in the IR portion of their website dedicated to "Corporate Governance." In this section, a company should present:

- A **governance overview**, including the roles of the chief officers and the independence of the Board of Directors

- The company's **"Code of Ethics,"** or a statement about why it does not have one, as required by the SEC. Updates, amendments, or waivers can be quickly reported here as well.

- The company's **Disclosure Committee** – its members and activities including review of filings and earnings releases, and creating and monitoring the internal control process for filing certifications.

- The company's **Audit Committee**, which is responsible for the appointment, compensation, retention and oversight of the work of any public accounting firm serving the company.

- Any **non-GAAP reporting** guidelines and policies

- **Director biographies**, if they are not elsewhere prominent on the site

4

Evaluating Whether Your Company Is Ready To Approach Wall Street

The objective of any investor relations program is to build a base of long-term investors who believe in a company and its management team. While some executives might hope that as part of this process their stock will appreciate, the truth is that the real aspiration should be that their stock will attain its highest intrinsic value. In reaching out to investors and communicating their stories, companies should strive to attract those investors that will become their partners, who will provide advice and capital access for the right ideas. This is best accomplished if a company understands its valuation, properly communicates it to the right investors, and then works to maintain and deepen these relationships as the company grows.

Many a management team jumps the gun and reaches out to investors before it is ready to do so. And, as can be seen in the case of Acme Corporation, considering the vulture like short-selling investors, this could result in more harm than good. Before a company concludes that it is ready to be proactive in its investor relations outreach and to approach investors, it is recommended that it complete the following 10-point checklist:

1. I know my current market value and have a business plan in place that will allow me to achieve a higher intrinsic value. **Yes/No**

2. With my business plan and growth strategy in mind, I have gone through the process of self-introspection and honestly know the investment proposition(s) that my company represents. **Yes/No**

3. I have compiled a list of investors whose investment profile includes companies with my company's investment proposition. **Yes/No**

4. From what I know of these investors' profiles, every investor on this list is able to purchase stock in my company. **Yes/No**

5. My communications platform contains all of those means of communicating contained in Chapter II and each is consistent with the other. **Yes/No**

6. Looking down on my communications platform from 25,000 feet above, any investor reviewing it (and without the benefit of commentary from management) will clearly understand my company's investment proposition. **Yes/No**

7. My company's website contains an investor relations section that includes all of those elements mentioned in Chapter III and is easily accessible and navigable from the home page. **Yes/No**

8. The investor relations section contains a corporate governance section with those elements mentioned in Chapter III. **Yes/No**

9. I make an effort to build relationships with my shareholders either by personal interaction or by providing a regular stream of information that

constantly reminds them of my company's business plan and growth strategy as well as our progress in executing on this plan. **Yes/No**

10. What keeps me awake at night is worrying about my business and executing on my business plan – not my stock price. I realize that the success of my business will ultimately be recognized by investors as they will attribute a value to my business representative of this success. **Yes/No**

Investor relations is an art – "the art of communicating value." It is not a science and no one method is better than the other. Nevertheless, this art requires a disciplined approach. While a company need not answer "yes" to all of the questions above to be successful in attracting new investors, only when it is able to do so, will it be able to truthfully say that it has done everything possible to achieve its highest possible intrinsic value.

ABOUT THE AUTHOR

Jeff Corbin serves as a Managing Partner of KCSA Worldwide and oversees the firm's investor relations department, both domestically and internationally. Recognized as one of the leading independent investor relations firms in New York City, KCSA represents more than 60 publicly traded companies in the United States, Europe and Mid East.

Mr. Corbin has been with KCSA for more than eight years. Prior to that he was a securities and corporate attorney in New York City, specializing in corporate reorganizations, bankruptcy proceedings, transactional matters and commercial litigation. He has lectured in the United States on the topic of building relationships with Wall Street as well as internationally on the subject of Wall Street's perception of foreign companies and what they must do in order to attract U.S. investors.

An alumnus of Cornell University where he received his B.A. in government from the College of Arts and Sciences, Mr. Corbin is a juris doctor from the Benjamin N. Cardozo School of Law.

He is a member of the Public Relations Association of America, the National Investor Relations Institute, the American Bar Association and New York Bar Association.

He currently lives in the New York City area with his wife, Suzanne, two daughters, Jessica and Alexandra and son, Gregory. Questions or comments regarding this book can be addressed to jcorbin@kcsa.com.

C-Level Quarterly Journal
What Every Executive Needs to Know

The objective of C-Level is to enable you to cover all your knowledge bases and be kept abreast of critical business information and strategies by the world's top executives. Each quarterly issue features articles on the core areas of which every executive must be aware, in order to stay one step ahead - including management, technology, marketing, finance, operations, ethics, law, hr and more. Over the course of the year, C-Level features the thinking of executives from over half the Global 500 and other leading companies of all types and sizes.

Management
Best Sellers

Visit Your Local Bookseller Today or www.Aspatore.com For More Informatio

- <u>Corporate Ethics</u> - Making Sure You are in Compliance With Ethics Policies; How to Update/Develop an Ethics Plan for Your Team - $17.95

- <u>10 Technologies Every Executive Should Know</u> - Executive Summaries of the 10 Most Important Technologies Shaping the Economy - $17.95

- <u>The Board of the 21st Century</u> - Board Members From Wal-Mart, Philip Morris, & More on Avoiding Liabilities and Achieving Success in the Boardroom - $27.95

- <u>Inside the Minds: Leading CEOs</u> - CEOs from Office Max, Duke Energy & More on Management, Leadership & Profiting in Any Economy - $27.95

- <u>Deal Teams</u> - Roles and Motivations of Management Team Members Investment Bankers, Professional Services Firms, Lawyers & More in Doing Deals (Partnerships, M&A, Equity Investments) - $27.95

- <u>The Governance Game</u> - What Every Board Member & Corporate Director Should Know About What Went Wrong in Corporate America & What New Responsibilities They Are Faced With - $24.9

- <u>Smart Business Growth</u> - Leading CEOs on 12 Ways to Increase Revenues & Profits for Your Team/Company - $27.95

- CEO Profit Centers – Top CEOs on Key Strategies for Increasing Profits Exponentially in any Economy - $27.95

Buy All 8 Titles Above & Save 40% - Only $131.75

Call 1-866-Aspatore (277-2867) to Order

Other Best Sellers

- Ninety-Six and Too Busy to Die - Life Beyond the Age of Dying - $24.95

- Technology Blueprints - Strategies for Optimizing and Aligning Technology Strategy & Business - $69.95

- The CEO's Guide to Information Availability - Why Keeping People & Information Connected is Every Leader's New Priority - $27.95

- Being There Without Going There - Managing Teams Across Time Zones, Locations and Corporate Boundaries - $24.95

- Profitable Customer Relationships - CEOs from Leading Software Companies on using Technology to Maxmize Acquisition, Retention & Loyalty - $27.95

- The Entrepreneurial Problem Solver - Leading CEOs on How to Think Like an Entrepreneur and Solve Any Problem for Your Team/Company - $27.95

- The Philanthropic Executive - Establishing a Charitable Plan for Individuals & Businesses - $27.95

- The Golf Course Locator for Business Professionals - Organized by Closest to Largest 500 Companies, Cities & Airports - $12.95

- Living Longer Working Stronger - 7 Steps to Capitalizing on Better Health - $14.95

- Business Travel Bible - Must Have Phone Numbers, Business Resources, Maps & Emergency Info - $19.95

- ExecRecs - Executive Recommendations for the Best Business Products & Services Professionals Use to Excel - $14.95

Call 1-866-Aspatore (277-2867) to Order